CONTENTS

KT-525-789

OUR ELECTRIC WORLD

BEFORE ELECTRICITY

One hundred and fifty years ago, machines that ran on electricity had not been invented. Houses did not have electric lights. People used candles or gaslights to see in the dark. You could not watch television or listen to a stereo.

Before electricity there were no electric cookers or microwave ovens, so cooking was done over an open fire or using a coal-fired stove.

There were no electric machines for farming or industry. Businesses depended on work done by hand, steam engines or using water for power. There were no computers and no email. Letters were written by hand with a pen and ink.

ELECTRICITY TODAY

Electricity is necessary to our lives today. It powers our homes, factories and schools. It lets us light up the streets at night.

Electricity helps us to communicate and share ideas and information instantly with people on the other side of the world.

All computers run on electricity.

CURRENT ELECTRICITY

Electricity is a form of energy. The type of electricity you use most often is called **current** electricity. This type can flow or move.

Imagine you have a piece of a plastic tube filled with marbles. If you make a circle from the tube and push one of the marbles 3 centimetres, then all the marbles will move just that much around the circle. The power of your push is passed from one marble to the next.

When you turn on an electric switch, the light comes on instantly.

An electric current flows in a similar way to this. It flows through a wire instead of a plastic tube. Instead of marbles, the wire is filled with tiny particles called **electrons**. Electrons carry an electric charge through the wire. The electrons, like the marbles, do not move very fast, but the electric charge moves at the speed of light. That is 300,000 kilometres (186,000 miles) per second!

▼ *Electricity is carried across the countryside by cables strung between pylons.*

ELECTRIC CIRCUITS

An electric **current** needs three things to work. First, it needs a path to move along, which is usually a wire. Second, it needs a source of electrical energy. One source of electrical energy is a cell, or battery, which stores **chemical energy**. This energy can be changed to electricity. The third thing that is needed is a **circuit** for the current to flow around. A circuit is like a circle. Electricity can only flow around a complete circle or circuit. If the circuit is broken, the flow of electricity stops.

This cable car in New Zealand runs on electricity and needs a very large electric motor to make it work.

All electric appliances need a source of electricity. Some things use batteries for their power. Larger electrical devices must be plugged into a socket to work.

A hairdryer needs to be plugged into an electric socket.

PROJECT

Make an electric circuit.

You will need:

a battery in a holder
two pieces of wire
a small lightbulb in a bulb holder.

1. Attach one piece of wire to one end of the battery and one side of the bulb holder.

2. Attach the other piece of wire to the other end of the battery and the other side of the bulb holder.

3. Does your bulb light up? If it does, you have made an electric circuit.

4. What happens if you pull one of the wires loose and break the circuit? The bulb goes out because the circuit is no longer complete.

USEFUL ELECTRICITY

electricity
pylons

power station

thick
wire cable

underground cable

Current electricity is very useful. It can be switched on and off very quickly. It can be carried along wires to where it is needed. Electrical energy can be changed into forms of other energy, such as light, heat and movement energy. The current electricity you use in your home comes from power stations. It is carried by wires and cables to where it is needed.

Electricity enters your home through a single cable, or bundle of wires. From here, wires carry current to every room in the house.

Each room has switches and sockets. We plug all the electric devices that we use each day into these sockets.

In a lightbulb an electric current flows through a thin wire called a filament. The filament gets so hot that it glows with a bright light.

CONDUCTORS AND INSULATORS

A British plug.

Some materials let electricity flow through them. These are called **conductors**. Others do not let electricity pass through them. They are called **insulators**. Conductors provide a path for electricity to follow. Insulators are used to keep electricity from flowing to places where it is not wanted.

PROJECT

Conductors and insulators.

You will need:
a battery in a holder

three pieces of wire

a small lightbulb in a bulb holder

objects made of different materials, such as a coin, a paper clip, a rubber, a key, a plastic pen, a glass bottle, aluminium foil and cardboard.

1. Make up the electric circuit using three wires as shown.

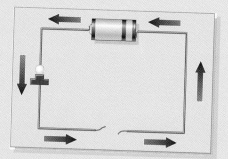

2. Check that it works by touching the two loose wires together.

3. Add each of the objects one after another to the circuit between the two loose wires.

4. Put all the things that let the bulb light up in one pile. These are conductors.

5. Put all the things that do not allow the bulb to light up in another pile. These are insulators.

What do the things in each pile have in common? What are they made of?

Electric cables, wires and plugs are covered by plastic or rubber. It is important to make sure these coverings do not become damaged.

An American plug.

All metals conduct electricity. If they do not, check to see if they are painted or varnished. Plastic and rubber are good insulators.

!

EXPOSED WIRES THAT CARRY ELECTRICITY CAN BE VERY DANGEROUS AND CAN GIVE YOU AN ELECTRIC SHOCK.

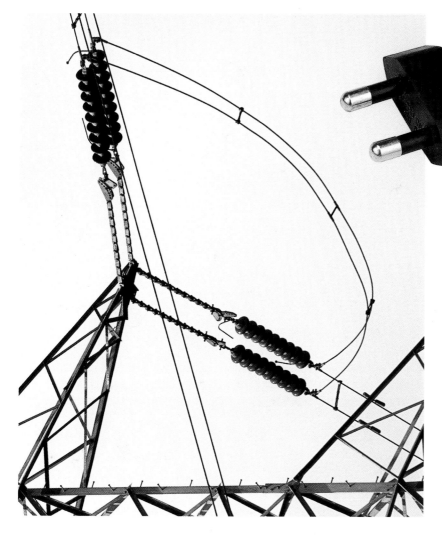

A European plug.

Water is also a good conductor of electricity. Never touch a light switch with wet hands. You could get a really painful shock.

◄ *Porcelain and glass are good insulators and are often used on electricity pylons.*

STATIC ELECTRICITY

One type of electricity does not flow along as a **current**. This is static electricity. Have you ever heard little snapping sounds or seen a spark when you took off your sweater? Have you ever got a shock when you touched something metal after walking on a rug? These things are caused by static electricity.

PROJECT

You can charge a balloon with static electricity.

You will need:

a woollen sweater

a balloon

some small pieces of paper or polystyrene.

Blow up the balloon and rub it on your woollen sweater to charge it with static electricity. Now try these quick experiments.

1. Hold the balloon against a wall in a warm, dry room.

2. Hold the balloon over the pieces of paper or polystyrene.

What happens? In each case, the balloon attracts the things because of its electric charge.

Static electricity is not very useful. In one way it can be quite dangerous. Lightning is caused by powerful static electricity formed in clouds during thunderstorms. Lightning can cause great harm. Because it usually takes the shortest route to the ground, tall buildings are most likely to be struck by lightning.

To reduce the chance of this happening, many tall buildings have metal wires going down their sides. These are called lightning **conductors**. If lightning strikes the top of the building, the electricity will flow safely down the metal rod to the ground.

AMAZING!
Between 1942 and 1977, a park ranger was struck by lightning seven different times. Amazingly he survived!

MAKING ELECTRICITY

Electricity is made using a **generator**. You may have a generator, or dynamo, on your bike. As the wheels of the bike turn, part of the dynamo also turns. The dynamo turns the movement energy, created by you, into electrical energy. This can be used to make the lights on your bike work.

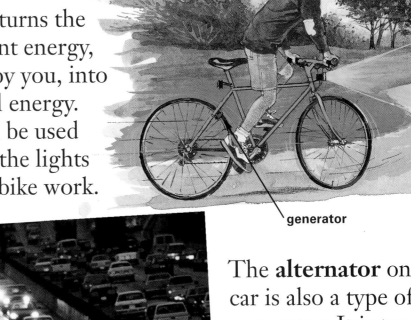

generator

The **alternator** on a car is also a type of generator. It is turned by the engine. This movement generates the electricity that powers the car's lights, heater and music system.

Cars would not be able to travel at night without electric lights.

ELECTRIC POWER STATIONS

Most of the electricity we use in our homes, schools, shops and factories is generated in power stations. Many power stations burn **fossil fuels**, such as coal or natural gas. The burning heats water to make steam. Moving steam is used to turn a large fan called a **turbine**. The moving turbine causes parts inside the generator to move and generate electricity.

These are the cooling towers of Fiddler's Ferry power station in the UK.

ELECTRICITY FROM WATER

Electricity can be generated from moving water, too. **Hydroelectric power** (HEP) stations use moving water to turn their **turbines**. HEP plants are often built in countries that have high rainfall and mountains with fast-flowing streams. Canada is the largest producer of HEP in the world, while Norway produces more than 99 per cent of its electricity from hydropower. Countries like Egypt and Zimbabwe in Africa have built large dams and produce a considerable amount of electricity this way.

Around 20 per cent of the world's electricity is produced by hydroelectric power. This HEP station is in Ffestiniog, North Wales.

ELECTRICITY FROM WIND

The power of the wind can also generate electricity. In California, USA, one wind farm has 300 wind turbines that supply electricity to the area around Los Angeles.

These wind turbines are part of a wind farm in California, USA.

ELECTRICITY FROM THE SUN

The Sun is also an important energy source. Energy from the Sun is called solar energy. The Sun's energy can be changed into electricity inside solar cells. This type of energy is useful. It is a clean source of energy, and one that will not run out like many other natural resources will.

MAGNETISM

WHAT IS MAGNETISM?

Magnetism is the invisible force of attraction or repulsion between some substances, especially iron. The result of this is that magnets can make things move without actually touching them.

bar magnet

ring magnet

horseshoe magnet

Most magnets are made from iron or steel and can be made into many different shapes.

You can make exciting sculptures with these magnetized shapes.

WHAT WILL A MAGNET ATTRACT?

The most magnetic material is pure iron. However, iron is rarely found in its pure form. It is usually mixed with other metals. Anything that has iron in it will be somewhat magnetic.

PROJECT

Try testing some objects to find out which ones are magnetic.

You will need:

a strong magnet

a group of objects to be tested: such as a metal spoon, a plastic ruler, a CD, a tin cup, a wooden spoon, a pair of scissors, a rubber.

1. Sort the objects into two groups. One group will be those that you think will be magnetic. The other will be those you think won't be.

2. Now test each group by holding the magnet over each object. If the object is drawn to the magnet, it is magnetic.

3. Write a list of the objects that are magnetic and another of those that are not.

Did you guess correctly? What does this tell you about some of the metals you tested?

MAGNETIC POLES

The ends of a magnet are called poles. Each magnet has a north and a south pole. Magnets are often labelled. The north pole is labelled N, and the south pole is labelled S. Sometimes magnets are painted so that the north pole is red and the south pole is blue.

A north pole will always be attracted to the south pole of another magnet. Two south poles will repel (push away from) each other. The same thing would happen with two north poles.

PROJECT

Magnetic poles.

You will need:
two bar magnets
two toy cars
a clear strip of tape
for fastening.

1. Tape a magnet to the roof of each toy car with the two south poles at the front of both cars.

2. If you roll the cars toward each other, the two south poles will repel each other. The cars will be pushed apart.

3. If you move one car up behind the other, the north and south poles will attract each other. You will have caused a crash!

MAGNETIC FIELDS

The push or pull of a magnet is called its magnetic force. Most of the force of a magnet is at its ends. However, the force spreads in all directions along the magnet. This space around a magnet, in which the magnetic force is felt, is called the **magnetic field**.

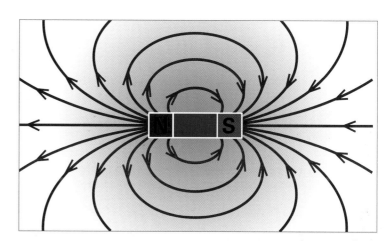

PROJECT

Look at a magnet's lines of force.

You will need:
a bar magnet
some iron filings, or shavings
a thin sheet of plastic or piece of paper.

1. Place the sheet of plastic or piece of paper over the magnet.

2. Shake the iron filings gently over the area where the magnet is.

3. Look at the pattern made by the iron filings.

MAKING MAGNETS

Some metals can be made into magnets. Try making a magnet.

PROJECT

You will need:
a strong bar magnet
a long steel nail
some paper clips.

1. First, test to see if the nail is magnetic. Does it attract the paper clips?

always move the magnet down the nail in the same direction.

3. Stroke it about 30 times. Now, see if it is magnetic. How many paper clips can it pick up? Try stroking it again. See if you can make it more magnetic. Will it pick up more paper clips?

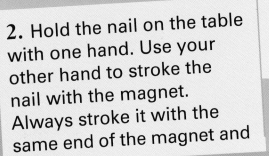

2. Hold the nail on the table with one hand. Use your other hand to stroke the nail with the magnet. Always stroke it with the same end of the magnet and

How does this work?

A magnetic material can be thought of as holding millions of tiny magnets. In a magnet, these tiny magnets all face the same way. In a material that is not magnetic, these magnets face in different directions.

By stroking the steel nail with a magnet, you started to line up the tiny magnets inside the nail in one direction. With each stroke of the magnet, some of the tiny magnets were pulled into line. The more you stroked, the more tiny magnets were lined up. The nail became a stronger magnet.

This nail has been magnetized.

non-magnetic nail

magnetic nail

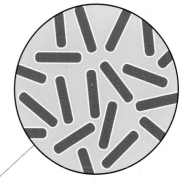

25

EARTH AS A MAGNET

Earth acts as if it had a huge bar magnet inside it. This is caused by the very hot, iron core at the centre of the planet. If there were a bar magnet inside Earth, it would have one end at the magnetic north pole. The other end would be at the magnetic south pole. The **magnetic poles** are not quite the same as Earth's geographic North and South Poles.

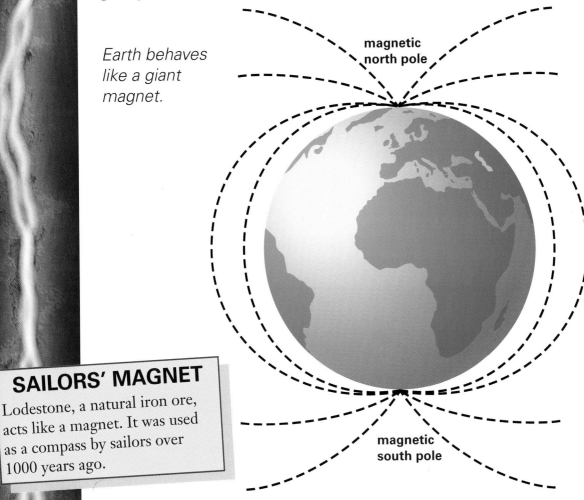

Earth behaves like a giant magnet.

magnetic north pole

magnetic south pole

SAILORS' MAGNET

Lodestone, a natural iron ore, acts like a magnet. It was used as a compass by sailors over 1000 years ago.

Lines of magnetic force run through Earth from one pole to the other. If it is allowed to turn freely, a magnet will align itself with the magnetic north and south poles. This is what makes a compass work.

PROJECT

Make a compass.

You will need:
a large needle
a small piece of cork or polystyrene
a magnet
a saucer of water.

1. First, you need to make the needle act like a magnet. You do this by stroking it with a magnet. Do this at least 20 times.

2. Now, stick the needle on the piece of cork or polystyrene.

3. Float it in the dish of water.

The needle will swing around to point in a north-south direction. This is what a real compass does.

A compass is especially important in helping ships at sea to find their way. Many drivers and hikers also use compasses to guide them.

ELECTROMAGNETISM

MAGNETISM AND ELECTRICITY

Magnetism and electricity are closely related. There are magnets in the **generators** that produce electricity. There are also magnets inside electric motors. An electric **current** can produce its own **magnetic field**. Electricity can also be used to create a magnet. Such magnets are called **electromagnets**.

PROJECT

Make an electromagnet.

You will need:
a battery in a holder
a long iron nail
some plastic-covered wire [about 60–100 centimetres long]
some paper clips or pins.

1. Wind the wire around the nail about ten times.

2. Attach one end of the wire to one terminal, or the connection point on the battery. Attach the other end to the other terminal.

3. Hold the nail over the paper clips or pins. What happens?

4. Now switch off the electric current by breaking the connection of one of the wires.

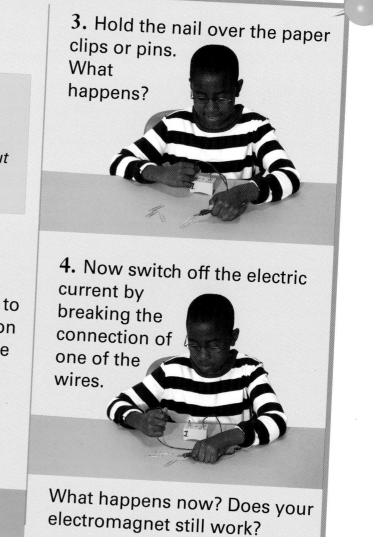

What happens now? Does your electromagnet still work?

The electricity flowing through the tight coils of wire creates a strong magnetic field from one end of the coil to the other. The force lines up all the magnetic particles in the nail and turns it into a magnet. The more coils of wire there are, the stronger the magnetic force.

Electromagnets are very useful because the magnetism can be switched on and off with the electricity. Electromagnets are found in many things in a house, such as televisions, telephones and doorbells.

Very strong electromagnets are used in scrapyards to move and sort scrap metal. The magnet releases its load when the electric current is switched off.

A magnetic train seems to 'float' above its track. Two sets of electromagnets hold it there. When the electricity is turned on, the train glides very smoothly along its track. There is no **friction** of the wheels on rails. As a result, these trains can travel much faster than ordinary trains. The train stops when the electricity is turned off.

GLOSSARY

alternator electric generator that produces an electric current

chemical energy energy stored in fuel

circuit path around which electricity can flow

conductor substance that allows electricity to flow through it

current flow of electrons through a wire

electromagnet magnet made by passing electricity through a wire wrapped around an iron core

electron negatively-charged particle

fossil fuels fuels formed over millions of years from the remains of living things. Coal, oil and natural gas are all fossil fuels.

friction force which slows down the movement of one surface against another

generator device that converts movement energy into electricity

hydroelectric power electricity produced by the movement of water

insulator material that does not allow electricity to pass through it

magnetic field space near a magnet where magnetic power can be noticed

magnetic poles two points on a magnet where the magnetic effect is strongest

turbine machine that is made to rotate to drive a generator

FURTHER INFORMATION

BOOKS

Electricity and Magnetism, Steve Parker (Hodder Wayland, 2000)

Electricity and Magnets, Sarah Angliss (Kingfisher Books, 2001)

Electricity: Where Does it Come From, Where Does it Go? Paul Humphrey (Franklin Watts, 2000)

My World of Science: Using Electricity, Angela Royston (Heinemann Library, 2001)

Science Topics: Electricity and Magnetism, Chris Oxlade (Heinemann Library, 2000)

WEBSITES

BBC Science pages – loads of interesting science stuff – regularly updated.
http://www.bbc.co.uk/science OR http://www.bbc.co.uk/schools (then select 'science')

Electricity – what is it, and how do we use it?
http://www.eia.doe.gov/kids/electricity.html

Explore Science – access a library of information on many science topics. Includes photos and artwork, video and animation, activities and tests.
http://www.heinemannexplore.com

Magnets – an invisible attraction – answers to common questions about magnetism and the compass.
http://www.science-tech.nmstc.ca/english/schoolzone/Info_Magnets.cfm

INDEX